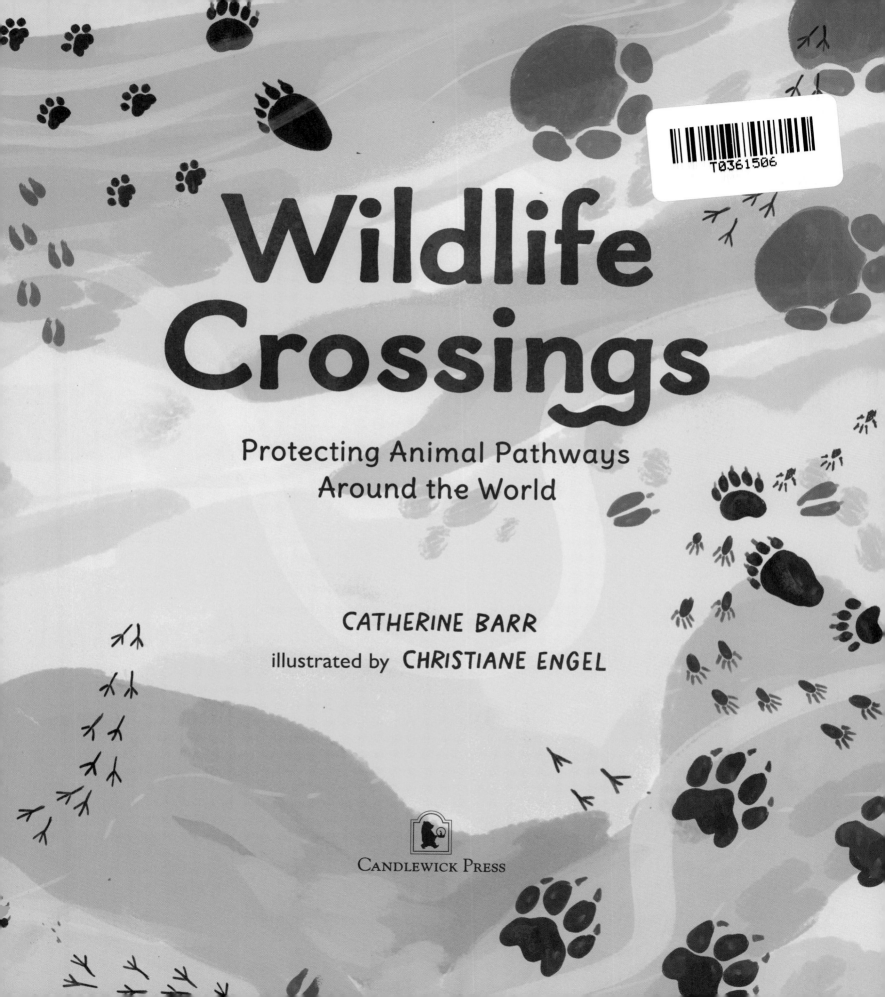

Wildlife Crossings

Protecting Animal Pathways Around the World

CATHERINE BARR

illustrated by CHRISTIANE ENGEL

CANDLEWICK PRESS

For Caz, for sharing her love of gibbons,
adventure, and friendship
CB

For Josie
CE

Acknowledgments

The author and illustrator would like to thank the following for their expert advice:

Trevor Kinley, MEDes, RPBio, Environmental Assessment Scientist, Parks Canada

Upasana Ganguly, Manager and Head, Right of Passage: Wildlife Corridors Projects, Wildlife Trust of India

Eric Wikramanayake, formerly Director of Wildlife and Wetlands, WWF, Hong Kong

Carolyn Thompson, BSc, MRes, PhD Researcher, University College London and ZSL's Institute of Zoology, UK

British Hedgehog Preservation Society and the People's Trust for Endangered Species

Beth Pratt, California Executive Director, National Wildlife Federation, US

First US edition 2024
First published by Otter-Barry Books (UK) 2024

Library of Congress Catalog Card Number 2023946119
ISBN 978-1-5362-3625-5

24 25 26 27 28 29 TLF 10 9 8 7 6 5 4 3 2 1

Printed in Dongguan, Guangdong, China

This book was typeset in Chewy and Gill Sans.
The illustrations were done in mixed media.

Candlewick Press
99 Dover Street
Somerville, Massachusetts 02144

www.candlewick.com

Contents

Wildlife Crossings
Linking Wild Spaces to Help Animals Survive

Our planet is crisscrossed by ancient paths—formed by endless journeys made by 8.7 million species searching for food, water, mates, and safe places to breed.

Wild creatures need room to roam. But often their paths are blocked because our human footprint is breaking nature apart. We are slicing up land with roads and destroying forests for cities and farms. Fishing gear is cutting across oceans, and fences run to the horizon to separate land.

People are turning habitats into isolated patches of nature, already under threat from climate change. As space is squeezed, tensions rise between wildlife and people.

Track the journeys of seven amazing animals. Discover why they are in trouble and follow their paths to find out how wildlife corridors are helping them survive.

3

Elephants in Trouble (India)

Elephants are wanderers, eating as they roam. In India, elephants cross huge landscapes, searching for water and food. As seasons change, elephant grandmothers lead their giant families toward the rains. They follow ancient paths to find greener grass, fresher shoots, and water holes filled by distant storms.

Elephants wade through local farmers' rice fields at the forest edge, which is dangerous for local people and ruins their precious crops.

The elephants' ancient paths are blocked by train tracks and busy roads.

But elephants' wild homes are shrinking. The patches of forest and grassland where they live are separated by roads, fences, farmland, and villages. When they find their paths blocked, hungry elephants raid farm crops, scaring villagers, causing chaos on roads, and getting lost.

If elephant families wander close to villages, local people make lots of noise to frighten them away—but younger elephants might run the wrong way and get lost.

The elephants are struggling to reach the distant water hole where generations of elephants have drunk, cooled off, and played.

Elephants love the smell of jackfruits, so they head off to find the villagers' jackfruit trees for a feast.

Children learn about local wildlife and paint elephant stories on school walls!

Elephant Corridors help elephants migrate

Elephant corridors are spaces that link elephant habitats, making it safer for elephant families to go on their journeys without being disturbed. These wildlife corridors make it possible for elephants to follow in their ancestors' footsteps.

Electric fences powered by solar energy keep elephants away from fields of bananas, maize, and rice.

It is not always easy to make space for giants. Scientists and local people are working hard to keep elephants on the move—in peace. Road signs warn drivers to look out for special places where elephants can cross the road. In schools, children are learning how to keep wandering elephants safe.

Can you spot 10 elephants?

Hedgehogs in Trouble (UK)

As dusk falls, hungry hedgehogs wake up and amble off to find food. They wander through churchyards, step onto streets, and stroll along hedgerows and across yards looking for bugs and worms.

But often their food forages are blocked by fences, roads, and walls. In these fragmented habitats in the UK, hedgehogs are in steep decline.

If people replace fences and forget to make a hole, hedgehogs can get trapped in yards.

In neat, tidy yards, hedgehogs struggle to find shady spaces like logs and leaf piles to sleep in.

Hedgehogs visit an average of eight yards in one night. But barriers like fences can keep them from roaming far enough to find food, a quiet place to rest, or even a mate.

In yards and in fields, pesticides are poisoning the slugs and insects that hedgehogs eat. In the countryside, hedgehogs like to hide in hedgerows, but these, too, are disappearing fast.

It is risky for hedgehogs to cross the road—they move slowly and don't look before they cross!

Hedgehogs can walk up to 1 mile/2 kilometers at night in search of food.

Hedgehog Highways help hedgehogs escape

Hedgehog highways link hog-friendly habitats with paths and holes. By making gaps in garden fences, fitting ramps over big steps, and creating holes in walls, people are reconnecting places so hedgehogs can roam.

These "Hedgehog Champions" are creating hedgehog-friendly communities in cities, villages, universities, and schools through the UK Hedgehog Street campaign.

More than 120,000 local people are helping to make hedgehog highways, connecting yards around the UK.

Mother hedgehogs may carry their babies, called hoglets, in their mouths to a safer place to rest.

There are lots of ways to welcome hedgehogs. Wilder yards and gardens offer places to hide, a shallow bowl of water provides a welcome drink, and **HEDGEHOG CROSSING!** signs on roads help alert drivers to keep hedgehogs safe.

Away from the traffic, these popular, prickly creatures prefer unplowed field boundaries, pesticide-free farms, and shelter in thick, shady hedges.

Hedgehog hospitals take in and look after injured, distressed, or underweight hedgehogs rescued from the wild.

Hedgehog Champions count hedgehogs by placing specially made tunnels in their path and tracking the tiny footprints they leave behind.

Can you spot 7 hedgehogs?

Birds in Trouble (East Asia)

RUSSIA

On long migrations, water birds need safe places to rest and feed. Their stepping stones are food-rich wetlands, where they refuel before flying on. Three million birds take a break on the Yellow Sea mudflats in Asia.

The spoon-billed sandpiper, or "spoonie," is one of the rarest shorebirds of all—it is threatened by the disappearance of wetland habitats.

CHINA

INDIA

Within weeks of hatching in the Arctic, spoonies fly south for 50 hours without stopping.

The shores of the Yellow Sea are drained to create dry land for buildings, factories, and farms.

The Yellow Sea is colored by sand from the Gobi Desert in China, but now pollution is turning it brown.

Spoonies spend winter on the mudflats of the Indian Ocean—but even here they face the danger of illegal netting.

ARCTIC OCEAN

Bird migration routes are called flyways. More than 50 million birds use the Asian flyways that spoonies use.

Flyways Around the World

PACIFIC OCEAN

NORTH AMERICA

To feed, spoonies sweep their spoon-shaped bills from side to side, slurping a muddy soup of worms, insects, and shrimp.

Migration stepping stones like lakes can also be a risky place to rest, as bird trappers may be waiting with nets. These invisible "mist nets" stretch for up to 1 mile/2 kilometers, catching hundreds of birds every day, mostly for food.

Illegal hunting, alongside the disappearance and pollution of wetlands, is pushing migrating water birds like spoonies to the edge of extinction.

Wetland Stopovers help birds rest

Bird lovers are working across continents to protect wetland stopovers on flyways around the globe. But as spoonie numbers plummet—there are fewer than five hundred left in the whole world—this little shorebird is getting extra help. Scientists are very carefully collecting eggs from spoonies' Arctic nests to hatch them away from predators. These spoonies are released into wild flocks that take a break on Yellow Sea mudflats.

Scientists are fitting tiny trackers to spoonies to map their journeys—this helps them work out where to protect these little birds.

Some coastal wetlands of the Yellow Sea are UNESCO World Heritage Sites, now protected for migratory birds and local people. Scientists are gathering evidence of habitat damage and falling bird numbers. This will prove that other wetlands on these shores must also be protected to save this important flyway stepping stone.

Healthy wetlands protect our coastal cities and shores from floods and stormy seas, made worse by climate change.

Wetland parks allow schools, families, and local people to discover the wonder of wetlands.

Can you spot 5 spoonies?

Gibbons in Trouble (China)

Gibbons swing high in the trees across the Asian forests where they live. They rarely touch the forest floor. But roads, logging, farmland, and towns, as well as natural disasters like mudslides, are breaking up their forest homes.

On Hainan Island in the South China Sea, the rarest gibbons of all face a massive forest gap—this one was caused by a natural landslide. Once there were two thousand Hainan gibbons living on Hainan Island—today there are fewer than thirty-five!

Forests are cut down to plant rubber trees. The rubber is then sold around the world.

Habitat destruction, caused mostly by human activities, threatens all 20 species of gibbon with extinction.

Like all gibbon groups, Hainan gibbons are cautious when crossing open ground. They fear big snakes like pythons as well as predators like humans and dogs. They are able to leap between isolated trees, but sometimes they hesitate and fall. Huge forest gaps and the breakup of forest habitats threaten the survival of gibbons and other primates around the world.

Gibbons get an electric shock if they grasp electricity wires slung near villages when trying to use them like trees to keep off the ground.

Development for the thriving tourist industry on Hainan Island threatens habitats where island wildlife lives.

Canopy Bridges help gibbons cross gaps

Scientists have discovered that apes and monkeys will use rope bridges to swing across forest gaps. But it takes time . . . Gibbons can take as long as six months to pluck up the courage to use the bridge at all. On Hainan Island, specialist human tree climbers are making canopy bridges to reconnect gibbon habitats. This helps the endangered apes find food and meet mates.

On canopy bridges, female gibbons often take the lead, using the rope as a handrail or swinging across.

Gibbons have really long arms that help them swing superfast across the canopy—they can leap farther than the length of a bus in just one swing!

Canopy bridges are made from rope and bamboo, so they are a cheap, quick fix. Beneath them, scientists and local communities are planting fast-growing trees to fill in forest gaps.

On Hainan Island, these newly planted trees are connecting smaller nature reserves. One day this will create a huge nature reserve so these gentle apes can not only survive, but thrive.

Camera traps catch these acrobats on film, showing scientists how often and how many gibbons use the ropes.

In other countries, too, skilled climbers are fixing rope bridges to help gibbons and other animals cross roads and forest gaps.

At dawn, ecotourists and local communities can hear gibbons singing in the canopy.

Can you spot 11 gibbons?

Fish in Trouble (Germany)

Some fish, like the Atlantic salmon, hatch in rivers and then swim to the sea, where they spend most of their lives. Incredibly, they return to the river where they were born to lay their own eggs. But around the world, their journeys upriver are blocked by dams. There are more than a million river barriers in European rivers alone—most make it impossible for fish to reach places to spawn.

Around the world, many dams were built to control rivers. They harnessed the power of water to make electricity and made it possible for big ships to use the rivers. But dams of all sizes change river habitats, alter the water quality, and stop fish from migrating upstream. In Germany, dams once made it impossible for salmon to reach places they sought to lay their eggs, so salmon died out in these rivers.

salmon

The journeys of eels, salmon, and trout are blocked by this dam.

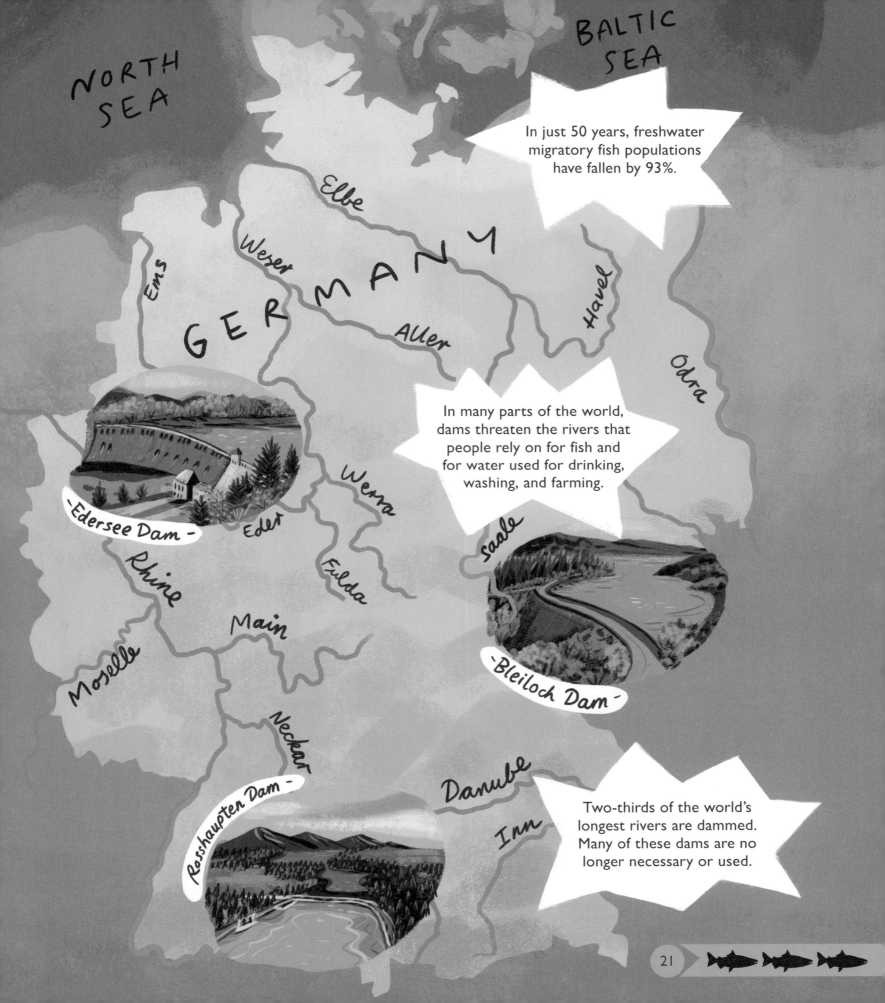

NORTH SEA

BALTIC SEA

GERMANY

Elbe

Weser

Ems

Aller

Havel

Odra

Werra

Eder

Fulda

Rhine

Saale

Main

Moselle

Neckar

Danube

Inn

-Edersee Dam-

-Bleiloch Dam-

-Rosshaupten Dam-

In just 50 years, freshwater migratory fish populations have fallen by 93%.

In many parts of the world, dams threaten the rivers that people rely on for fish and for water used for drinking, washing, and farming.

Two-thirds of the world's longest rivers are dammed. Many of these dams are no longer necessary or used.

Fish Ladders help fish swim upriver

Atlantic salmon migrating up a tributary of the Rhine in Germany meet many gigantic dams. But here on the Moselle River in Koblenz, a fish ladder helps them up and around. They swim from pool to pool past the dam before swimming on upstream to lay their eggs. Fish ladders like this reconnect river habitats. They help migrating fish make their long journeys to shallow riverbeds to spawn.

Unable to jump up the dam, salmon use this fish ladder in the Moselle, where they leap from pool to pool until they get upstream.

Fish ladders are expensive to build and not all freshwater species are able to use them, but they are helping species like salmon, sturgeon, and shad.

Fish will return to make their journeys if old, unused dams are removed. Thousands of dams are now being torn down so wildlife in these rivers can return. Free-flowing rivers carry soil to floodplains, estuaries, and beaches. This protects wildlife habitats as well as people and buildings from floods, storms, and rising seas driven by climate change.

Salmon are now being reintroduced into Germany's rivers, including the Rhine, which was once Germany's most important salmon river.

Fish are important in freshwater food webs at all stages of their life cycle. Eggs and young fish provide food for other creatures, whereas adult fish are predators, feeding on shrimp, mollusks, and insect larvae.

Can you spot 7 pink salmon?

Bears in Trouble (Canada)

Grizzly bears raise their cubs in forests and alpine meadows in the Canadian Rocky Mountains. In this remote landscape, mother bears show their cubs how to sniff out and discover juicy berries and grubs to eat. But they must also teach them how to cross a dangerous road. A wide highway cuts right through their protected land.

Animals crossing roads are dangerous for drivers, too, especially at night, when it is difficult to see.

It takes a lot of time, energy, and money for national park rangers to remove dead and injured animals from the road.

The tiny long-toed salamander crosses the road to reach ponds to breed—they make this risky journey every year.

Traffic on the Trans-Canada Highway brings millions of visitors to Canada's famous Banff National Park. They come to explore the mountain landscape and discover its amazing wildlife. But this busy highway threatens the lives of bears, moose, deer, cougars, and long-toed salamanders as they search for food or mates on the other side of the road.

Where roadsides are unfenced, grizzly bears may attempt to cross, but they often turn back. They must be brave and lucky to miss fast-moving traffic.

Bear Bridges help bears cross the road

Bear bridges over Canada's longest road, along with the tunnels underneath it, were some of the world's first wildlife corridors. Moose, elk, wolves, and grizzly bears prefer wide open bridges where birds and butterflies fly overhead in the quieter sky space. But black bears and big cats head into cool, dark tunnels built beneath the highway.

Bear hair samples prove that both grizzly and black bears use the crossings.

Coyotes cross first, while bears take longer to use these green bridges.

Wildlife crossings in Banff have dramatically reduced the number of animals killed on this road.

Fences along the road on either side of wildlife crossings funnel animals toward the safest place to cross.

Animals might avoid the bridge if they smell humans, so only Parks Canada scientists are allowed to get close.

Satellite collars, remote cameras, and animal tracks show scientists exactly who is on the move and where. This tracking proves that the forty-four bridges and underpasses in Banff National Park are a success. Hundreds of thousands of creatures, from tiny insects to bears and their cubs, are safely crossing in both directions each year.

Can you spot 5 bears?

Cougars in Trouble (USA)

As human populations grow, some big cats have adapted to human spaces. There are two megacities in the world where big cats live within city limits: Mumbai in India and Los Angeles in the United States. One cougar even lived under the famous HOLLYWOOD sign, hiding by day and hunting by night. Cougars, also known as mountain lions, roam across the state of California.

As people take up more space, some wild animals, like cougars, are forced to live closer and closer to urban areas.

28

HOLLYWOOD

Close to the sparkling city of Los Angeles, the Santa Monica Mountains National Recreation Area is carved up by busy multilane highways. It is almost impossible for wildlife to cross these roads to find food and mates. But one cougar became famous for dodging cars, trucks, and human detection while on a 50-mile/80-kilometer trek that included two major freeways. National park staff named the big cat P-22.

Wildlife park rangers look through thousands of camera-trap photographs to spot and track a cougar on the move.

Camera traps and GPS tracking help people figure out where wild animals go, map the places they are trying to explore, and learn which roads they are trying to cross.

Cougar Crossings help cougars survive

Scientists fit radio tracking collars to big cats to understand their movements and help keep them safe. But when cougar P-22 crossed the 101 and 405 freeways, he was not wearing a collar. Instead, scientists used DNA testing to confirm that the same animal had made all these crossings. This led to a campaign, supported by local people, for a wildlife crossing to join up the Santa Monica Mountains National Recreation Area.

This wildlife crossing will be made of special materials to reduce traffic noise and deflect bright lights in order to encourage animals to cross the road.

So far 43 US states have wildlife crossings.

On either side of the crossing there will be special soundproof walls so that wild animals won't be frightened by the noise and bright lights of constant traffic.

The Wallis Annenberg Wildlife Crossing will be the biggest wildlife crossing in the world. It will allow Californian wildlife to cross the 101 freeway to reach wild spaces in a busy urban area. Coyotes, skunks, deer, raccoons, lizards, and even black bears might wander across. All of these wild creatures need space to find mates and food while living on land that they share so closely with people.

The 300,000 people who drive under the bridge each day will see that green crossings help people live alongside all kinds of wildlife, including bigger predators.

Can you spot 4 cougars?

Meet Seven More Species rediscovering ancient paths

Badgers on Ecobridges in the Netherlands

Linking two forest areas, Natuurbrug Zanderij Crailoo is a super-long wildlife bridge for deer, badgers, and other wild animals. This animal highway crosses a railway line, a sports complex, and busy roads. It is the longest wildlife overpass in the world so far (although the Wallis Annenberg Wildlife Crossing will be the longest once construction is completed).

Beelines Join City Gardens in Norway

From flowers in window boxes to rooftop gardens and vegetable plots below, the city of Oslo in Norway is helping bees. People in the city are helping to create pollen highways so bees can feed as they fly across the city. Schools are joining in, creating feeding stations for hungry bees.

Crab Bridges on Christmas Island

In the wet season on this Australian island, 14 million crabs crawl out of the forest and migrate to the ocean. Bridges with special crab-friendly surfaces help them reach the ocean to mate. Each female will then lay up to 100,000 eggs!

Elephants Going Underground in Kenya

While trucks hurtle past overhead, African elephant families in Kenya amble underground through a specially built tunnel to avoid the road. The tunnel links more than 2,000 elephants in the Kenyan highlands with elephant herds in the plains and forests below.

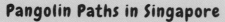

Jaguars Crossing Central and South America

Local communities and conservationists have ambitious plans to create a jaguar corridor. These big cats live in 15 unconnected landscapes across Central and South America. The corridor aims to reconnect tropical wetlands and great forests so jaguars are free to roam.

Pangolin Paths in Singapore

Sunda pangolins can wander between nature reserves in Singapore thanks to the Eco-Link@BKE, a wildlife bridge. It used to be very dangerous for this endangered scaly mammal to journey across the road in search of food, mates, and shelter. Birds and monkeys also now prefer to cross using this growing rainforest bridge.

Tigers Under Treetop Highways in India

Tigers, wild dogs, bison, and porcupines can safely cross under the raised highway in Pench Tiger Reserve in India. Special fences guide wildlife to underpasses that help keep the wild animals in this forest reserve on the move.